# THE JOEL MANUSCRIPT

## JO HAMMERS

The Joel Manuscript

Copyright © 2011 by Jo Hammers

All rights reserved. No part of this book may be reproduced or transmitted in any form or by any means without written permission of the author. For information, address Paranormal Crossroads & Publishing, Po Box 5056, Bella Vista, AR 72714.

ISBN 978-0-9849879-0-0

www.paranormalcrossroads.com

This work is fiction. All of the characters, organizations, and events portrayed in this novel are either products of the author's imagination or are used fictitiously.

The publisher does not have any control over and does not assume responsibility for author or third-party Web sites or their contents.

The scanning, uploading, and distribution of this book via the Internet, or via any other means without permission of the publisher is illegal and punishable by law. Please purchase only authorized electronic editions and do not participate in or encourage electronic piracy of copyrighted materials. Your support of the author's rights is appreciated.

Image copyright George Nazmi Bebawi, 2011 used under license from shutterstock.com.

# Table of Contents

1. Introduction — 7
2. Chapter One — 11
3. Chapter Two — 14
4. Chapter Three — 19
5. Chapter Four — 23
6. Chapter Five — 28
7. Chapter Six — 31
8. Chapter Seven — 32
9. Chapter Eight — 33

# THE JOEL MANUSCRIPT

## JO HAMMERS

# INTRODUCTION

## *JOEL SPEAKS TODAY*

1. My name is Joel. I live and speak again.
2. I am one of the ancient perfected ones who lived a life on Earth as a foreteller or prophet pointing the way for those of clouded minds to what was coming in future generations.
3. I have returned to speak to you, but in another form. I am that I am.
4. I am one of those who sought and reached perfection and enlightenment.
5. I am as GOD is.
6. My former words and prophecies were for those of the Old Testament and New Testament dispensation.
7. The Old Testament age is passed. The New Testament Age is ending.
8. You now exist in an over lapping of the New Testament Age and The New Age Dispensation or Heaven.
9. You stand with wings outspread ready to crossover with one foot in the New Testament Age and the other in the New Age Dispensation.
10. Heaven is now. The rapture is now.
11. Only those seeking higher knowledge which is God will be caught away into the Heaven that men have dreamed and fantasized about.

## Jo Hammers

12. The called will leave their stance in the New Testament Age and step their spirit man in to God's New Heaven.
13. The old is passing away as you read this.
14. I was a simple man named Joel who prophesied and died as an Earth human.
15. Everything that I saw, pointed to an age far advanced and different than the one I lived in.
16. I pointed men of darkness to a new religious experience and the laying down of their own.
17. I foretold the pouring out of the anointing on the New Testament Age and the great master prophet, Christ.
18. I spoke the latest in spiritual thought. I was New Age in my thinking for my day. I was the cutting edge.
19. I had one foot in two different dispensations. I stood in the over lapping, the catching away from the old to the new.
20. I was the chosen prophet, the rebel who dared to foretell the future and upset the thinking of my time.
21. I heard and answered my trumpet call to be a forerunner of a new age.
22. I was the prophet, the rebel, the speaker of new words and the pointer of my fellow man to what God was going to do in the future.
23. Now the time has arrived to speak once more.
24. God's New Day and Words are not in the past and its writings. He speaks today!
25. His words are coming forth from the trumpets and voices of modern prophets pointing you to a new dispensation beyond the New Testament Age.
26. I was once a prophet, a rebel prophet, the modern thinker for my day.
27. I pointed men standing in the Old Testament Age to the coming of the New Testament Age.
28. It is time to walk forward one more time and leave the old behind. There is a time of overlapping or crossing between dispensations.
29. Men stand with one foot in the old, and one foot in the new.

# The Joel Manuscript

30. The crossing between the New Testament Age and the New Age Dispensation is marked by the catching away or the rapture.
31. It is a time to lay the old down and rapture.
32. You must think yourself over from the New Testament age to the New Age Dispensation.
33. Many will be left behind because they are looking outside their human bodies for a physical flight to Heaven where they will lay around on clouds and rest in rocking chairs.
34. The rapture is of the mind thru thought.
35. Those rising in perfect thought experience the rapture or the catching away.
36. God is knowledge, perfect knowledge. To know God is to think.
37. To be caught away or to rapture is to rise in spiritual knowledge until we have perfected our inner man, the one who thinks.
38. Now is the time of the crossing over. The rapture is within you.
39. The rapture is laying down your old error thoughts you em braced in the New Testament Age and be willing to embrace the new.
40. Seek higher thought. Higher thought is Heaven! Higher thought is God!
41. This is the trumpet sounding your call to come up higher, to be as God is.
42. God is knowledge! It takes a perfect man of knowledge to know a perfect God.
43. Seek perfection and enlightenment.
44. Abandon your errors in thought.
45. Abandon the stifling religion that has a rope around the neck of your spirituality.
46. I am a citizen of the Great White City of the Perfected, the enlightened throng of Knowledge.
47. In your human world, I am the words you read.
48. Words are knowledge and knowledge is God.

**Jo Hammers**

49. I am one voice of the Trumpet. I am one of the perfected.
50. The New Testament Age is ending for you because this is your rapture call.

The prophecy of Joel for the New Age and those dwelling in the short overlapping time period between the New Testament Age and the New Age of Enlightenment or Heaven.

# CHAPTER ONE

## *JOEL SPEAKS FROM THE ALL KNOWING PLACE OF GOD*

1. I, Joel, have perfected myself and speak from the all knowing place of God.
2. Hear me, you aging speakers of a passing dispensation. Listen, all dwellers of the planet Earth. Has the catching away to God happened in your day? Has it happened in the days of your fathers now gone?
3. I tell you that the New Day of God has arrived. Pass the word, aging speakers to your followers and tell them to tell their children and friends and for them to pass on the word of kingdom come to all they know.
4. Great errors in religious thought have been fed the men of Earth who have in turn fed them over and over birthing darkness of thought in generation after generation of those seeking spiritual ways.
5. Open your eyes, men of religious movements embracing church doctrines as absolute truths and are drunk with the idea that they are the chosen, the only group acceptable. You have been blinded by your leader's sugar coated words. The silver tongued, sweet orators of errors will no longer be tolerated.
6. A New Dispensation of the enlightened of God is now growing in strength and is prepared to speak devouring

like a lion the darkness of thought produced by spiritual errors.
7. The old denominations and religions of the world will be stripped of their spiritual men. Left will be dark, blind followers embracing error who will be cast away into the spiritual land of dark endlessness. A new tree, a new dispensation of light seekers will grow.
8. Seek with tears and the laying down of darkness to fill your soul with the all knowing perfection of God.
9. Old ways of approaching God thru men and leaders of un perfected states of soul will no longer be honored by God. Spiritual leaders of the passing dispensation will grieve because God has forsaken them in their errors and non-dedication to seeking perfection and enlightenment.
10. The old realms of religious thought will cease. Their base of followers will grieve the fall and death of their doctrines. The spirit and the anointing will lift from them.
11. The keepers of the flocks of men will be ashamed of their dead religions. The workers in their groups will grieve for those appointed to them and the ones they have drawn in. The salvation harvest of the New Testament age has come to an end.
12. The Earth gatherings of many vines or religions will falter seeing their doctrines exposed as errors. The many religions of the world, like trees, will wither and die from within. The light of God, the joy of knowing perfect truth will be absent.
13. Study, strengthen your soul, and seek with tears and dedication God's new move. Leaders of the many religious gatherings abase yourself laying down your doctrines and your errors in thought and deed. Your approach and path to God has ceased. The old is passing away as you read this prophecy.
14. Call a fast, the laying aside of all doctrines and religious beliefs. Call the oldest and most experienced of religious leaders and then the followers to a time of embracing the

idea that God has abandoned the old and that a new dispensation with perfection and knowledge as its standard has arrived. Join together and seek the new day and enlightenment.
15. Cry""""Holy-Holy-Holy!" having eyes to see God's new move. Those not having eyes to see will suffer the discarding of God.
16. God's new move will bring with it the ceasing of the gatherings of religious men being fed. The anointing and light, the food of God, will cease. A spiritually hungry man is an unsmiling one.
17. Men have rotted in the filth of their imperfection. Their gathering places are gone. Their collected errors of thought have failed, because darkness is failure.
18. Why does man in his error groan. Why do the gatherings of error followers beg to be lead and to be fed? Why? There is no grazing place for their souls. The congregations of darkness have died for lack of light.
19. To the Infinite of Light, I will turn. The burning away of the wilderness of dark thought and the standing prophets or leaders of it has came to pass
20. Men of darkness have turned looking up to the perfected as the flowers in a drought thirst for rain. The old springs of dark thought are dried up.
21. Dancing light has devoured the allure of the dark watering holes of the wilderness of thought.

# CHAPTER TWO

## *HEAVEN COMETH AND NOW IS*

1. Speak the New Dispensation call in Zion where you stand. Make the ears of the followers of light take note. Let all those searching for light in man built gathering houses tremble at the call to change, to abandon. The New Day of Perfection, Heaven cometh and now is.
2. The arrival of perfection and light, God's new day and move, is a day of darkness and gloom to those not seek ing. The change will be fog to the thinking of those of darkness, clouds they can't see thru. They will be lost in the whirlwinds of change. A multitude of serious seekers will climb and stand on the mountains of God. The turning to perfection and enlightenment's call will be the major event of many generations of men.
3. Light burns away darkness. The perfected will torch away darkness of thought as they walk forward. Behind, they leave men with the burning desire to serve enlightenment's call. Where their words are heard, light will reign. Darkness can't escape the power of consuming enlightenment and perfection.
4. The perfected of the New Dispensation will be powerful and capable of spreading the light being greatly flexible in their words and abilities.
5. They shall be chariots of fire delivering their words and move from gathering place to gathering place, from podium to podium. Their words calling men to perfection

# The Joel Manuscript

will be thoughts of burning fire, cleansing and preparing men to battle their inner darkness till they are perfect light.

6. The words of the perfected orators of the New Dispensation will cause men to cringe in pain seeing their errors of thought. The hearers will become a hungry face wanting to be filled.

7. The heroes of enlightenment shall run with the truths of perfection like an army going to war. Everyone will have their place and because of perfected states, ranks won't be broken.

8. The perfected ones will not put down his brother. All will walk their paths in perfect union. They shall enter mirrors of righteousness, the unreal, but not be harmed by deceit.

9. They shall enter into the gathering places of men. They shall run upon their built walls of error spreading light. They will be permitted to speak in the houses of the gatherings. They shall present their truths and like a thief snag men's attention away from darkness.

10. In their presence, Earth men will tremble. They will cause higher thoughts to snag the thinking of men. The old natural thinking, the proclaiming and discarding of doctrines will cease. The old leaders and orators of non-perfected states will cease to be in acclaim.

11. God's voice and the call to enlightenment will be the trumpet sound of his army of the perfected. His men of truth are divine in comparison to ordinary men. They are powerful and will speak for God and execute judgment. The arrival of God's New Dispensation of Perfection will be great to those seeking light. It will be invasion and destruction to those embracing darkness. Who of darkness can tolerate a light invasion? Who of the light can tolerate darkness? Who will stand?

12. God speaks now saying, "Seek my perfect enlightenment, my knowledge with your every breath and thought. Cry for light. Weep for your need of perfection. Mourn for

your deadness of spirit"
13. Outward holiness will not gain you entrance to God's New Day and Dispensation. Turning from dark errors of thought and heartless, cold decisions will face you toward the entrance of God's Gate of Holiness. God is gracious, merciful, patient, to those turning to lay darkness down.
14. Darkness of thought is doomed. The wise dark man will turn and hope for a chance to change even in the hour of doom. Perhaps in God's mercy He might hear him and let him be the last man to climb to perfection. There will be a last man.
15. Speak the voice of God in Zion, the gathering of the perfected. Call a time of soul searching.
16. Gather together those seeking perfection and call them to inner sacrifice. Call the eldest perfected ones of Earth's assemblies to attend. Gather the newest of perfection seekers and those of baby learning states. Let the sharing of perfected truth cause mature souls of perfection to spring forth.
17. Knowing that there are many steps in the climb to enlightenment and perfection and that the new seekers and the ancient perfected ones do not all share the same step, the priests will intercede for those of mixed stages of perfection saying, "Spare us as an unperfected people as we stand at your altar seeking to be so. Do not cast out our new seekers of lower baby stages. Give them time to rise in knowledge even though they are late in stepping to climb up the ladder of the Holy altar.
18. God loves his people down to the one on the lowest rung of the ladder who are climbing. The man standing idle on the bottom rung, he does not. The idle are a shame to God! The dedicated climbers he loves.
19. God says to those of his heart, "I will send you spiritual food, drink and anointing. You will be filled with them and I will not laugh at your naive walk in front of the ancient perfected.

20. I will remove from you the frigidness of soul. The dark words of men have frozen you in doctrines of error. They will be abased because they were proud to delay your path.
21. Fear not, climbers, rejoice because God has caused light to be victor over darkness.
22. Fear not, you unperfected leaders of evangelism. The truths you do know and have planted will spring forth multiplying themselves. The man perfecting himself and the gatherings of those like him will stand in the congregation of maturing growing souls.
23. Children of the call to perfection rejoice, be happy of soul because you sought out the teacher and the steps to perfection. NOW IS THE TIME OF THE LATTER RAIN! God's powerful anointed former rain fell once before. NOW IT FALLS AGAIN.
24. The gathering places of the perfected will be filled with orators speaking forth spiritual truths. The anointing will fall once more and the thirst for God's spirit will be quenched.
25. I will restore to the seeker the years wasted in darkness eating errors of thought. Error of thought is a plague which will bring about the destruction of dark souls.
26. The seeker of enlightenment, the knowledge of God, will be given all he can eat to the point of overflowing. You will acclaim to others the lifting of your soul to higher heights. Honor the God of your higher calling. Those seeking perfection will not be turned away.
27. You shall know that God dwells amongst the perfected, the new Israel, as supreme. Those seeking perfection will not walk in darkness forever. Sooner or later they become what they seek.
28. It shall come to pass in the day of the seekers of perfection; GOD WILL POUR OUT OF HIS SPIRIT ON ALL MEN ENTERING THE NEW DAY, THE NEW AGE OF PERFECTION. BOTH MALE AND FEMALE HUMANS WILL BE COME WALKING ORATORS, speakers,

messengers carrying the call to perfect one self and become Knowledge. The ancient ones TRAVELING IN HUMAN VEHICLES will walk between worlds traveling in dreams. The young arrivals to perfection will see VISIONS, ways of carrying knowledge into the future.

29. Upon those serving and leading the masses of seekers I will anoint. I will anoint their staff.
30. Great truths will fall upon the gathering of the perfected as well as those men just beginning to seek. Outside, the gatherings of dark souls will find that their spiritual eyes will start to cloud and death will pluck their eyesight.
31. The light of truth once extended to all men will cease. In the errors of darkness, men's souls will die as the Great Dispensation of the Perfected arrives.
32. Those who turn to God's Perfect Way will be saved. In Mt. Zion and the New Gathering of the Holy, the climbers to perfection will stand. A last residue of men will hear the call to come up higher.

# CHAPTER THREE

## *IN THE VALLEY WHERE ENLIGHTENMENT IS NOT*

1. In the New Dispensation Age, I shall let the blindness of error thoughts hold in bondage those once called mine and those of the former Jerusalem for a season.
2. God will bring the gatherings of error thoughts together down in the valley where enlightenment is not. There he will sound one last call to the masses in error to walk away into God's New Day. Scattered around the world in every nation are the once chosen spiritual leaders who have succumbed to darkness. God hasn't forgotten those who were once his chosen.
3. Errors of spiritual thought have grasped hold on those of the New Testament Age. The young thinkers are confused. The truths of perfection have been discarded for addictive flowery words.
4. What significance does errors and flowery words have in the presence of perfection, God. Cities of darkness will you speak against a straight walk of Holiness and Perfection? To attack the perfected is to bring it calling at your door.
5. Error has enticed many great and extremely great spiritual

men. It has carried them away into gatherings of degradation, error's meeting houses.
6. Error will sell your soul into slavery to demanding task master religions. You will find yourself in dark lands where the knowledge of God doesn't shine.
7. God is capable to start a man climbing toward enlightenment from the darkest pit of error. He is able to destroy darkness from within error's walls.
8. A dark place of cease to be exists for those of total darkness. When the last man answers his call to the light, men of darkness will enter their own far off land of cease to be appointed by God.
9. Proclaim this amongst the peoples, the enlightened. Prepare to battle with the orators of error. Present your strongest of the perfected to speak. Gather together light forces. Let all the ancient in truth gather.
10. The time of plowing and planting seeds is over. Now is the time of the fierce cutting away of darkness and the pointing out of dark errors. Let the new in the land of knowledge proclaim their truths learned. Let the weak say they are strong.
11. Proclaim who you are in your path to perfection and enlightenment. Join with like forces of light. Darkness will flee from you.
12. In the valley of understanding, God will judge the peoples for their adherence to the seeking of light.
13. Speak tongues with the sickles of reaping. Now is the end of darkness and a passing dispensation. Come you of perfections call and look upon men dying in darkness of error thought. Dark orators have multiplied the wickedness in men.
14. Worldwide seekers who have embraced errors of thought are in a time of sinking into further darkness. God's New Day is here. The land of spiritual cease to be awaits those sinking into error of thoughts.
15. GOD'S KNOWLEDGE, ONCE AVAILABLE DAY

AND NIGHT, IS BEING WITHDRAWN FROM THE NEW TESTAMENT AGE. Once great shining spiritual speakers presented a call to holiness and salvation. The call is ceasing.

16. God shall no longer be gentle with man. He shall be heard from the gathering of the perfected ones' voices. Those of the perfected and those climbers from Earth will hear and be stirred in soul. God shall be the leader of the perfected and the hope of those still climbing in truth. He will be the foundation of New Israel rising in spirit form.

17. You, reading this prophecy, will know God as He is. He will dwell in Zion, the holy mountain of His perfected who have risen to higher heights. The New Jerusalem, a city of the perfected will reign. Errors will not pass thru the minds that are perfected. They are the gates to the city and the New Age Dispensation.

18. It shall come to pass in the New Dispensation of God that those having answered their call to come up higher in thought shall speak sweet words. Those below will receive higher truths fed to them as the milk for a baby. The anointing will once more flow thru the gatherings of men seeking spiritual understanding. A great speaker from the gathering of the perfected will present truths and the call to come up higher to the skeptical mockers causing them to drink and spring forth.

19. Passing world religious persuasions will become unattended. The wilderness of dark thoughts will be destroyed. They will see a falling away because they chose not to lift their congregations higher. They took new seekers and let them starve from lack of spiritual food.

20. Zion's gathering shall stand in their perfected thought for ever. The Holy White City of God, the New Jerusalem, a place of perfected knowledge, will be passed down generation to generation..

21. God will sweep with a final cleansing the last seekers and then dwell in His people, the New Perfected Zion. There

is a beginning. There is an end.
22. The New Testament Age is coming to an end as you read this.
23. It is time to cross over. The catching away is here.
24. Rapture and seek God as He is. He is KNOWLEDGE and HIGHER THOUGHT.
25. The time to think and consider is now.
26. The spirit man that lives within you holds the key to the portal to Heaven.
27. He is the one that will step into the wind of the catching away.
28. The wind is within you.

# CHAPTER FOUR

## *THE CALL COMES TO HE WHO IS READY*

### THE CALL OF JAMES THE PROPHET

A man we will call James, a fast food worker, goes outside to take a break and sits down on a bus bench in one of the United States largest cities. It is not his intent to catch the public transportation. He just needs a place to sit and think.

James feels that his life is going nowhere except down the drain of life. He expected more from life than flipping burgers. The recession has forced him, like a lot of other educated men, to take a job not in his field. He has a college degree and minister's credentials. In his thinking, flipping burgers is a serious step down life's ladder. He has fellow ministers and Bible college friends who are doing the same.

James' graduation from seminary did not land him the church pastor ship that he dreamed of or a Christian post of some sort in the religious world. He was a burger flipper. He was ashamed of who he was because he knew that he was called. However, the religious world he wanted so much to be a part of had rejected him. Older experienced pastors were chosen ahead of him when he went to try out for different church positions. He was discouraged.

The night shift was about over, he had two hours left to put in. Sitting on the bench taking a break in the wee early hours of the morning as the sun was about to come up, a stranger in painter's whites walked up and sat down on the bench next to him.

"What you seek is passing away. With it will go many seasoned ministers full of their own prejudices and dark doctrines .Many of them will not be caught away to God's New Day. The Age of salvation for men is ending. The catching away is now happening as I speak." The stranger stated looking down the busy street. "Many men of religion travel the road to nowhere."

James turned to look at the stranger sitting next to him all dressed in white, "Do I know you?"

"I am the trumpet of God calling men to the rapture, the catching away to God's New Day. The call has now been presented to you. It will only come once," he stated.

"If the rapture is taking place now as we speak, then you and I are in deep trouble. We have both missed it!" He replied.

"I have not missed it. I am its trumpet. You may miss it if you ignore the sound of my voice." The stranger replied. "Men are rising all around you while you sink into a pit of despair a place of darkness, Hell on Earth."

"I have a call. No one hearing me seems to comprehend it. I have been turned down and turned down for various pastor positions. I am flipping burgers to feed myself, my wife, and two children. I know God can't be pleased with me in this going nowhere job. I am called to pastor and lead a people."

"That you are, but not of the dark men drowning in error of

thoughts and teachings. You are called to come up higher and be the voice of God in a new dispensation. The old religious world as you know it will cease to be when the catching away ends. There will be another Testament, the writings of those who are caught up into higher thought and then walk as spirit men between worlds. Have you considered that you might be called to be and write a book for The New Age Holy Bible, a testament beyond the King James New Testament?"

"You are serious, aren't you? I can see it in your eyes. You think the rapture is now?" he asked listening to the stranger.

"Now is passing for you. You have longed to hear the voice of God, but question it when it comes to you."

"You want me to dump my religious affiliation and begin again, like a new Adam entering a new Garden of Eden?"

"Yes. Many are called, but few choose to answer the sound of the trumpet's call. This is your opportunity and only one will be given."

"Why aren't my feet leaving the ground if this is the rapture?" James asked.

"It is not your physical body that will rise. It is the spirit man that lives in your body. Physical bodies are like vehicles. They get old, dented, worn out, and the motors quit. We as spirit men walk in and out of these human vehicles. It is the spirit man in us that rises. God is knowledge. He is not a human vehicle. He is a spirit being just like the one that lives in your human body. God can enter a human body if He wishes. He has appeared to man over the centuries in many forms. However, He is not the form. He is the spirit in the form. He is intelligence, a perfect intelligence. When we rise in perfect knowledge or thought, we rapture. We rise in thought or in the All Knowing. The act of being called away or going to Heaven is the gathering of spirit men who have became perfect in intelligence or thought. Spirit men can rise from their bodies and join with other spirit men in the higher realms of intelligence, and then return to earth to their bodies. This is the going and the coming again." He added,

"So the catching away will come like a thief in the night because it will only be the thinkers the open minded that will see it?"

"That is correct. You are called to think, to rise higher, too become knowledge which is God. Mad men may try to destroy your physical vehicle that you travel in on the Earth plain. However, once you perfect yourself in Knowledge you will be able to step your spirit man from one body to the next. The spirit man in that physical body you travel in is the real you. He can rise from the dead vehicle. He can also return to the dead vehicle or a new vehicle. This is the going away and coming again that the dedicated of the age of salvation, those perfected in Christ as well as the perfected of the new age will perform as normal daily events? If you think and perfect your spirit man, laying down all darkness of thought, you become the all powerful knowledge that God is. You become a part of Him. All the parts put together become Him!

"Am I being called to speak, prophecy, and point men to a new time period or dispensation where perfected men will step from their physical bodies and travel between two plains, Heaven and Earth at will?" he asked.

"Yes, you are called to be a prophet pointing men to the next dispensation. You stand in the time of the crossing over. The end of time or the end of the Dispensation of Salvation is beneath your feet. It is not in the far off future somewhere. You straddle a fence. That fence is the crossing over between the New Testament Age and the New Age Dispensation of Higher

Thought, or God. You, like me, are the Voice of God heralding its arrival. YOU AND I ARE WALKING BOOKS, THE FIRST BOOKS OF THE NEW AGE DISPENSATION BIBLE. I am the Trumpet. I am Genesis II. You are the book of James, the gate between the old and the new. Whoever enters your gate of knowledge are the men you are to lead. You will pastor a new gathering of the perfected and lead them into the new dispensation or Heaven. You are Moses in a new wilderness leading men out of darkness of thought, which is bondage. You are not called to pastor one of the New Testament Age dying denominational churches that are being abandoned by God. You are called to the New Dispensation and its gatherings!"

"Where will I find these followers of new thought?"

"They will come to you one by one. Lead them by day and feed your physical body how you will at night. All must work and provide for their physical means on Earth. The job is unimportant. It is being a part of a major dispensation change that is important. You are called to be the prophet known as James!"

James turned for a moment to glance at his job's back door where he heard one of the fast food cooks yelling his name. When he turned back, the Trumpet was gone. He had heard the trumpet sound of the catching away. It came unexpected as a thief in the night and those around him were unaware of its sound.

# CHAPTER FIVE

## *THE RAPTURE OR CATCHING AWAY*

1. There is a trumpet blowing, The END TIME CALL TO COME UP HIGHER.
2. The catching away to God and His Heaven is happening now as you read this.
3. It is not a physical flying off planet Earth to somewhere glorious in the sky seen by human eyes.
4. The rapture is of the soul, the spirit man who lives in your physical body.
5. Willingness to have an open mind and to think are the wings of the spirit.
6. When a soul seeks to know God who is Knowledge, he or she rises in enlightenment or the catching away.
7. A perfect state of knowledge, knowing all that God knows, is Heaven.
8. However, it is not the one that men want. Men seek an easy escape, a free hand out Heaven.
9. Heaven is not a lazy place of rocking chairs and fluffy clouds to sleep on.
10. Heaven is not a welfare state. Heaven doesn't tolerate those who don't work to get there.
11. Heaven is achieving a perfect state as a spirit and then joining the throng of others who have climbed one run of

the ladder at a time laying down all sins, errors in thinking, and deeds.
12. Heaven is being with God and the Perfected ones.
13. A lazy man cannot enter there. Laziness is a sin. Sin cannot enter there.
14. A perfect man in the eyes of God is one that has labored for his position in the Kingdom thinking and becoming all that he can be.
15. A lazy man wanting an easy heaven to fly away to is a stench in the nostrils of God.
16. You will not find in the Kingdom of Heaven those of death bed repentance.
17. All men are given free will choice and a life time to labor and perfect themselves of error.
18. A man of death bed repentance wants an easy slide into the back door of the land of the perfected ones. It doesn't work that way.
19. New Testament Age salvation will buy the man of death bed repentance a ticket to Paradise or the astral shore and no further.
20. The judgment seat of God is in paradise or on the astral shore, the place of arrival.
21. Death bed salvation will get you that far but no further.
22. All men are judged for their works, their labor, and their seeking of God who is knowledge.
23. The man of death bed repentance will be found wanting because he has nothing to present as evidence that he was striving for perfection which is the ticket to Heaven beyond paradise.
24. Many men with tickets to paradise will be judged and sent to the land of Cease To Be, the discarding place of lazy men and those refusing to use their free will choice to climb to perfection.
25. God condones no sin or those who want to try to slip into an easy door or window in to the land of the perfected, Heaven.

26. Death bed repentance is for thieves trying to find a quick window to get in at.

# CHAPTER SIX

## *SALVATION AGE ENDS*

1. With the ending of the New Testament Age, salvation by Christ also ends. Salvation has been a ticket to the judgment seat.
2. When the trumpet call ends, there are no more free tickets to the judgment seat.
3. The trumpet sound has fell on your spiritual ears as you have read this call to God's new day.
4. The age of salvation has ended for you.
5. Being caught away in thought and knowledge is your only portal to Heaven.
6. A man who is too lazy to open a book or consider higher thought will be the spiritually poor by choice, lazy men.
7. They will want the perfected to let them in the back door for a warm up or a free meal.
8. Heaven is not a welfare state. It is the land of the perfected.
9. There will be no salvation in the New Age Dispensation at the hand of another.
10. Every man must climb or not climb.
11. Perfecting oneself is a die, sink, or swim experience.

# CHAPTER SEVEN

## *THE CATCHING AWAY IS NOW*

1. The rapture, the catching away is now.
2. Hearing this message ends the salvation New Testament age for you.
3. This is your call, your trumpet sound.
4. Heaven can only be accessed by your inward man.
5. Seeking Heaven within points you to Heaven's gates.
6. Heaven is not in the far off sky seen by human eyes.
7. Only the spirit man traveling in your human body can experience and see the rapture or catching away.
8. You, a spirit man that lives in your human body, can rapture or go to God in thought.
9. God is not a being of form like the human body, although he can take form when he wishes.
10. God is knowledge and only your spirit man can access him in that form.
11. Seek the perfecting of your inner man and go to commune with your God.
12. You have heard the call to rapture in thought and knowledge.
13. You are accountable for your journey.
14. There is a land of cease to be for souls who are useless, lazy, and fails their life lesson of using free will choice for the perfection of the soul.

# CHAPTER EIGHT

## *A MESSAGE FROM A SON OF GOD, A BROTHER OF THE MASTER*

1. I AM A PERFECTED ONE AND TRAVEL BETWEEN HEAVEN AND EARTH IN SPIRIT FORM.
2. On Earth, I travel in a human body. In Heaven I am a spirit, a mist and need no form.
3. I am knowledge just as God is knowledge.
4. I have chosen to perfect myself in Him.
5. I travel between Heaven and Earth as the angels do.
5. Christ was a perfected one traveling in a human vehicle.
6. We, the perfected go and come again as he did.
7. Perfection is the standard of Heaven.
12. All men dwelling there are measured by it.
13. This is your trumpet call. Step your spirit man from your body in thought and become as he is, perfect.
14. You have been chosen for a ticket. However, you must pay the price for that ticket.

www.ingramcontent.com/pod-product-compliance
Lightning Source LLC
Chambersburg PA
CBHW061316040426
42444CB00010B/2666